Disney · PIXAR
Annual 2006

Editor: Martin Shubrook
Art Editor: Phil Williams

Published in Great Britain in 2005 by Egmont Books Limited, 239 Kensington High Street, London W8 6SA.
All rights reserved. Printed in Italy. ISBN 1 4052 2102 X
The term OMNIDROID used by permission of Lucasfilm Ltd.

Note to parents: adult supervision is recommended when sharp-pointed
items, such as scissors, are in use, or hot water is required.

1 3 5 7 9 10 8 6 4 2

This book belongs to:

Name: lewis welch

Age: 11

My favourite character is:

Dash

Disney · PIXAR

Annual 2006

Contents

How it began

Years ago, one Super stood out from the crowd. He captured the toughest villains and protected the world from evil in the only way he knew how ... by using his Super strength!

Then, suddenly, the heroic acts of the Supers seemed to cause more trouble than good – people didn't want them any more. Mr. Incredible and his friends were forced to give up their extraordinary lives and live undercover as regular civilians. They were never allowed to use their Super powers again.

For many years Mr. Incredible tried to live an ordinary life as Bob Parr. He got a normal job and tried his best to behave like a normal human being. However, at home, Bob and his Super family often found it very difficult to

keep their Super powers hidden. Every dinnertime turned into a Super fiasco!

Mr. Incredible desperately missed his life as a Super and often met with his Super friend, Frozone (who had changed his name to Lucius).

Bob would tell his wife that he and Lucius were going bowling but really they would sit in the car and listen in to the police radio. They were on the lookout for any crimes that they could help stop or any dastardly criminals they could catch.

Then, one day after being fired from his job, Bob opened his briefcase to discover a tiny computer hidden inside. Bob looked puzzled as a female voice came from the small device.

"Hello, Mr. Incredible," the sharp voice said. "We have need of your unique abilities."

Not suprisingly, Bob was a little suspicious. However, he missed the Super life so much that he decided to take the challenge.

Bob knew his wife, Helen, would never let him risk the family's undercover status by going back to work as a Super, so he told her that he was being sent to an out-of-town work conference. Then, in secret, he dressed in his old Super suit and before long, Mr. Incredible had boarded an ultra-sleek jet and was on his way to a lush volcanic island – an island called Nomanisan.

Aboard the jet, Mr. Incredible was told more about his mission.

"The Omnidroid 9000 is a top-

9

secret, prototype battle robot. Its artificial intelligence allows it to solve any problem with which it's confronted," said Mirage, the mysterious woman whose voice he had heard earlier.

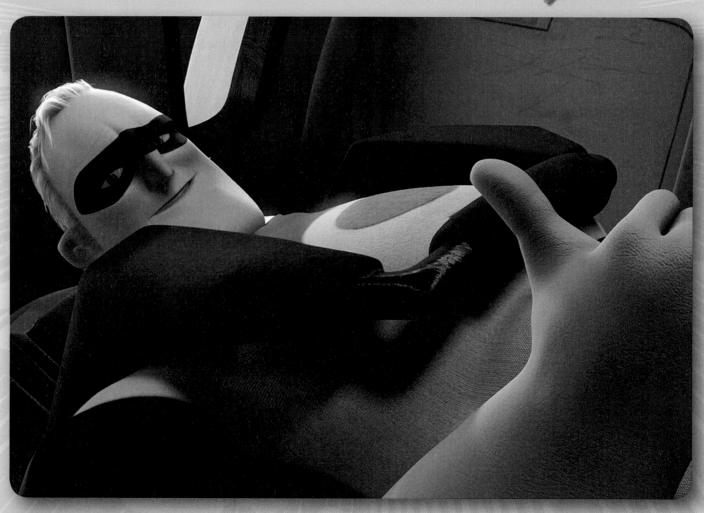

"So, let me guess," Mr. Incredible interrupted. "It got smart enough to wonder why it had to take orders?"

"Yes. We lost control," Mirage nodded. "Can you help?"

"Of course I can," replied Mr. Incredible. "Just show me the way."

Moments later, Mr. Incredible was dropped into the tropical jungle on the island of Nomanisan. Suddenly, he heard the sound of a tree being split apart. Mr. Incredible turned around and there was the Omnidroid, standing high above him. The giant hunk of steel with robotic spider legs battled against Mr. Incredible. It was stronger than Mr. Incredible could have imagined but he fought hard and outsmarted the giant robot by climbing inside its main body, tricking the Omnidroid into destroying itself!

Mr. Incredible's mission was accomplished. He was a Super again. Just as well, as an evil villain was not far away – Syndrome!

The end

Family ties

Can you help Mr. Incredible and Jack-Jack reach Dash and Elastigirl on the far side of the maze?

Start

Finish

Colour crazy

The Incredibles and Frozone are celebrating another victory. Can you add some colour to this picture?

12

Code cracker

Can you help Mr. Incredible crack this code? Use the KEY below to help you.

A=1 B=2 C=3 D=4 E=5 F=6 G=7
H=8 I=9 J=10 K=11 L=12 M=13 N=14
O=15 P=16 Q=17 R=18 S=19 T=20 U=21
V=22 W=23 X=24 Y=25 Z=26

2 5 23 1 18 5!
19 25 14 4 18 15 13 5
9 19 22 5 18 25
3 12 15 19 5.

Answer: BEWARE! SYNDROME IS VERY CLOSE.

Dodging Syndrome

The Supers are trying to escape from Syndrome. Play this game with a friend to find out who will be the first to escape from Syndrome and make it to safety.

You will need: a counter for each player and a dice.

How to play

Place your counter on either Mr. Incredible or Frozone. Take it in turns to roll the dice and move your counter clockwise around the board. If you land on Syndrome you must miss a turn. The first player to travel once around the board is the winner.

Omnidroid attack

The city of Metroville was in deep trouble! Syndrome had launched a rocket with a new, improved Omnidroid on board and it was heading straight for the city. Syndrome had a clever plan to terrify the people of Metroville with the Omnidroid, and then arrive on the scene and defeat the robot himself. The city would think *he* was a true Super and glory would be his!

Soon, the Omnidroid arrived and began its attack. Syndrome was secretly controlling the robot as it caused havoc across the city. But then, Syndrome realised he had a big problem, his plan was beginning to fail.

The Omnidroid was no longer taking his orders and the city was in big trouble. The robot was so smart it had decided it didn't like taking orders

from Syndrome, so it knocked him out and rampaged out of control!

The Incredibles arrived on the scene in the nick of time. Together, they tried to stop it but even with Frozone's help they couldn't defeat the menacing robot. Then, Mr. Incredible remembered the one thing that could defeat it. The only thing that could destroy the Omnidroid was the Omnidroid itself!

The Incredibles pulled together and used the Omnidroid's remote control unit to rocket one of its own claws straight through its centre. A great blast of fire rocketed from the robot and it fell to the pavement and exploded. The true Supers had saved the day! The city was safe.

However, the day was not over yet. On returning home, Helen opened the door to their house to find the babysitter had gone and Jack-Jack was in the arms of someone else ... Syndrome! His eyes glinted with evil as he fired his jet boots. Syndrome shot through the roof with Jack-Jack in his arms as he launched into the sky.

But it turned out that this sweet baby had his own powers that not even his parents knew about.

With a little help from his family, Jack-Jack escaped Syndrome's clutches, leaving the villain defeated once and for all. They truly were a most incredible family!

The end

17

Stretching shadows

Only one of the shadows on the right matches the big image of Elastigirl. Can you work out which one it is?

Answer: d

Dynamic differences

At first glance, these two scenes may look identical but there are ten differences in the lower one. Can you spot them all?

Answers:

Come home, Buster!

1

The toys were playing in Andy's room when they heard Buster barking. They climbed up to the window to see what Buster was so excited about, and saw that the garden gate had been left open. "That critter could get into some serious trouble out there," gasped Jessie. "We've got to get Buster back into the garden quickly," said Buzz.

2

"You guys keep watch, while I go into the garden and call him in," said Woody. He crept downstairs and tiptoed into the garden. "There goes one brave toy," said Buzz.

3

Woody peered around the garden gate and saw Buster sitting on the pavement. "Here, boy!" called Woody. But just then, a car drove past and Buster sprinted after it.

4 "Oh, no! Buster thinks it's fun to chase after cars," gulped Woody. He watched in horror as Buster stopped running after the first car and began chasing after another!

5 "Buster is going to get hurt if we don't do something soon," said Jessie. "But Woody can't leave the garden in case he's seen," said Buzz. "Someone do something!" cried Rex.

6 Woody kept calling Buster's name, but Buster was having too much fun to listen to Woody. "We can't leave him out there, playing in the traffic," said Buzz.

7 "If that crazy dog won't listen, we'll have to try something different," announced Buzz. He dug around in the toy box until he found what he was looking for.

8

"If Buster likes chasing cars, we'll give him a car to chase!" said Buzz. He stood at the window and steered RC, the remote control car, out of the garden and into the street.

9

Buster spotted the car and chased after it. Buzz guided the car back into the garden. "Nice driving, Buzz!" cried Woody and he carefully shut the gate behind Buster.

The end

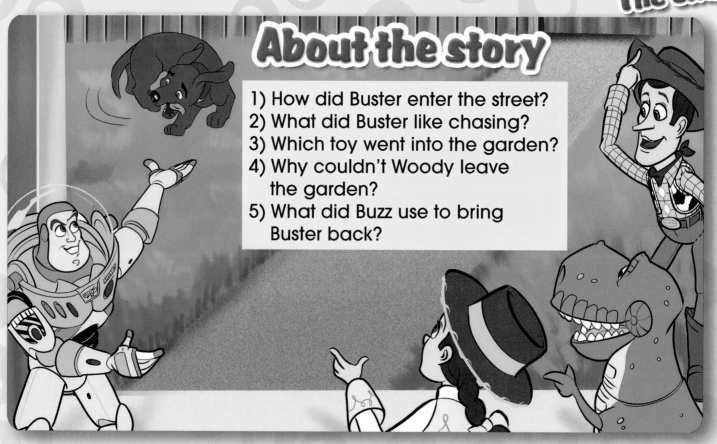

About the story

1) How did Buster enter the street?
2) What did Buster like chasing?
3) Which toy went into the garden?
4) Why couldn't Woody leave the garden?
5) What did Buzz use to bring Buster back?

Answers:
1) Through garden gate. 2) Cars. 3) Woody. 4) In case he was seen. 5) The remote-control car.

22

Reaching Woody

Can you lead Buzz through the maze to reach Woody? Be careful you don't run into the evil Emperor Zurg along the way!

Start

Finish

Etch's sketches

There are all kinds of things going on in Andy's room.
Join the fun and see if you can answer these questions.

1 Etch has been quick on the draw. Can you join the dots to see what he has drawn?

2 How many stars can you count?

3 Which two images of Rex match exactly?

A

B

C

D

E

F

4 Can you unscramble the letters below to find two of Buzz's friends?

R M E H
A M X

Galaxy duel

Who will be the winner in this cosmic blast out game?
You will need: a coin, a pen and plenty of courage!

How to play

Decide who will be Buzz and who will be Zurg. Take turns flipping the coin. If it comes up heads, colour in one of the blast spots on your opponent. If it comes up tails you have missed and must wait until your next turn. The first player to colour in all their opponent's blast spots is the winner!

Skater Buzz

Leap into action by adding some bright colours to this picture of Buzz flying through the air!

28

Planet puzzlers

Have a blast with Buzz by finding the answers to these two puzzles.

 Can you unscramble the letters to find four intergalactic words?

teplan rcekot

sart omon

2 How many spaceships can you count on this page?

Shuttle launch

Make your very own space shuttle.

You will need: a cardboard tube, white card, black card, kitchen foil, a black pen, scissors and glue.

1 Cut one end of the tube at an angle. Then, tape a circle of white card over each end of the tube.

2 Roll a cone shape from white card and tape it to the angled end of the tube.

3 Paint the whole shuttle white.

4 Cut some wings and a tail from white card. Decorate and glue to the shuttle body.

Note to parents: adult supervision is recommended when sharp-pointed items, such as scissors, are in use.

5 Roll some small cone shapes from black card and glue to the back of the shuttle.

6 Finally, glue on some foil squares for the windows and add markings with a black pen.

NOW YOU'RE READY TO FLY!

Groovy dancing

1

Everyone was excited because it was the evening of the Monsters, Inc. summer ball. "I expect to see every member of staff dancing tonight," chuckled Mr Waternoose.

"You won't be able to stop me," Mike giggled as he grabbed a mop and twirled across the Scare Floor. "Celia and I will dance until dawn."
Sulley watched Mike and groaned.

2

"What's wrong, big guy?" asked Mike. "I can't dance and I'll look really silly if I try," gulped Sulley. "Don't worry, pal, I'll teach you some of my fancy moves," said Mike, confidently.

3

But when Sulley tried to copy Mike's moves, he became twisted up and fell over. "No problem, we'll just find a dance that you're comfortable with," explained Mike.

4 Mike tried teaching Sulley every dance move he knew but Sulley was terrible at them all! "You've got less rhythm than a sack of wet sand," gasped Mike, feeling completely worn out.

5 "I'll never be able to dance," sighed Sulley sadly, and returned to his work. Sulley decided to stop thinking about learning to dance and concentrated on being scary.

6 Sulley opened the door and leapt straight into the room with his favourite scare routine, The Jump-and-Growl. Sulley pounced and spun with ease across the child's bedroom.

7 "Another perfect performance," laughed Sulley, when he returned to the Scare Floor and saw the full scream canister. "It's a pity you don't dance as well as you scare," said Mike.

8

Sulley thought about what Mike had said and grinned. That night at the ball, Mike was amazed when he saw Sulley march straight on to the dance floor and start dancing. When the other monsters saw Sulley, they raced on to the dance floor and joined in. "That's a great dance, Sulley, what's it called?" asked Mike. "The Jump-and-Smile," replied Sulley, with a grin.

The end

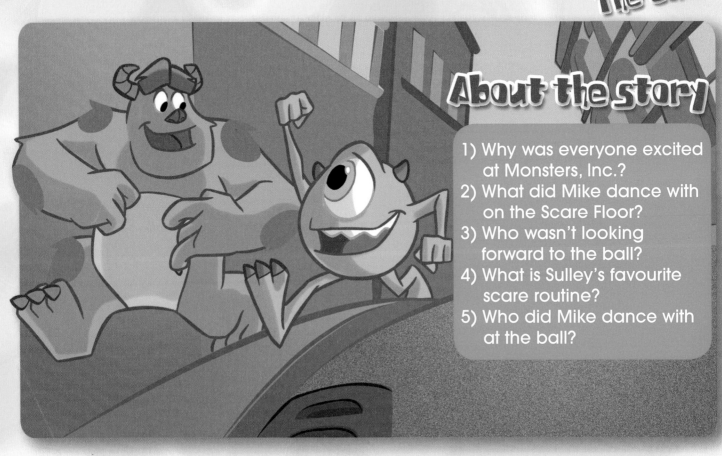

About the story

1) Why was everyone excited at Monsters, Inc.?
2) What did Mike dance with on the Scare Floor?
3) Who wasn't looking forward to the ball?
4) What is Sulley's favourite scare routine?
5) Who did Mike dance with at the ball?

Answers:
1) The summer ball was that evening. 2) A mop. 3) Sulley. 4) The Jump-and-Growl. 5) Celia.

Monster message

The Scare Floor noticeboard is telling the monsters to do something. Using the key at the bottom, can you work out what it says?

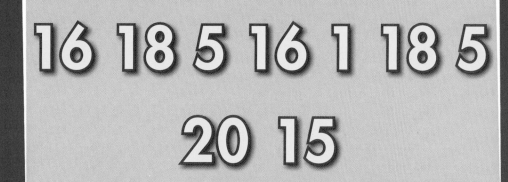

16 18 5 16 1 18 5

20 15

19 3 1 18 5

a- 1	b- 2	c - 3	d- 4	e- 5
f - 6	g- 7	h - 8	i - 9	j - 10
k - 11	l -12	m-13	n - 14	o - 15
p - 16	q- 17	r -18	s - 19	t - 20
u - 21	v - 22	w -23	x - 24	y - 25
				z - 26

Answer: Prepare to scare.

35

CDA alert

Answer:

1) Letters in wrong order on CDA agent's backpack. 2) Monsters, Inc. logo is upside-down. 3) Missing CDA agent on ledge. 4) Extra CDA agent at the window. 5) Part of the centre map is reversed. 6) Missing eyehole on CDA agent's suit. 7) Missing light on CDA agent's backpack. 8) Colour of CDA agent's light on backpack. 9) Colour of CDA agent's boot. 10) Colour of end of probe.

Lean on me

Mike and Sulley are taking some time to relax. Can you add some colour to this picture?

Socks and doors

Sulley knows that being a top Scarer takes great skill. Play this game with your friends to find out who has the skill to reach the full scream canister first.

You will need: a counter for each player and one dice.

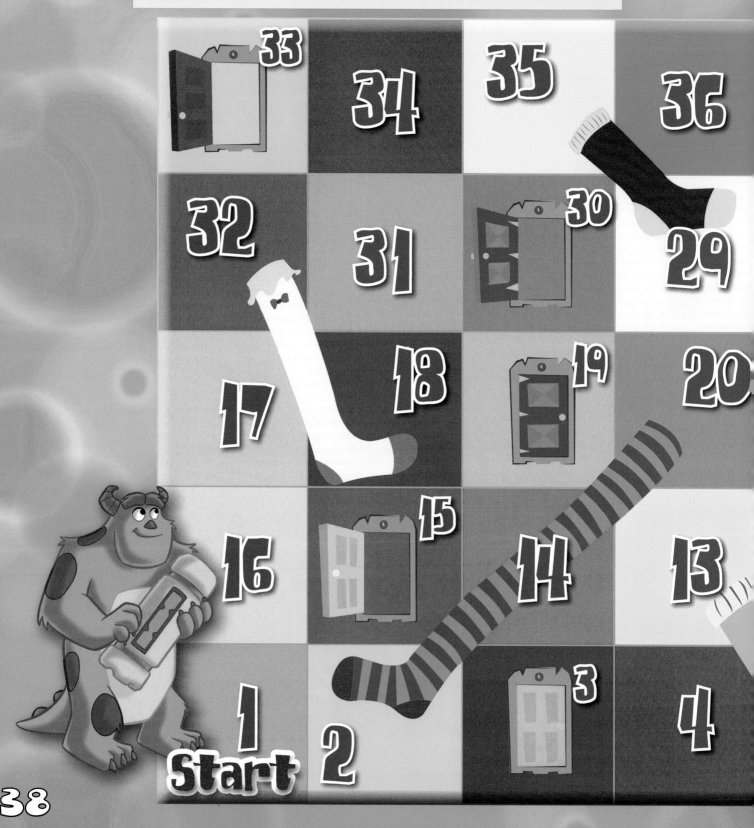

How to play

Place the counters on "Start". Take it in turns to roll the dice. Move forward the number shown. If you land on a closed door move your counter up to the matching open door. If you land at the top of a sock slide all the way back down to the foot of that sock. The first player to reach the scream canister is the winner!

37
38
39
finish
40
28
27
26
25
22
21
23
24
12
11
10
9
5
6
7
8

Goodbye, weeds!

One sunny Sunday morning, Sulley and Mike were hard at work in their garden. They were trying to pull up all the horrible, ugly weeds.

"We should be relaxing on our day off," grumbled Mike.

"We can relax once these weeds are gone," said Sulley.

"Gone? We've been out here all day and we're not even half finished," puffed Mike.

"I guess we'll just have to carry on next Sunday," replied Sulley.

"Oh great! Another day off where I'll be breaking my back instead!" complained Mike.

The next morning, Mike felt very stiff from pulling up the weeds. "I can hardly move," he grunted.

"Come on, Buddy, we're going to be late for work," said Sulley.

By lunchtime, Mike felt even worse. His muscles were so sore that he couldn't even leave the Scare Floor to go to the canteen.

"Mike, I've smuggled in an apple for you," whispered George, and he put a big shiny apple on top of Mike's work station.

A passing CDA agent saw the apple and thought that it looked like a child's ball. He quickly pressed the child contamination alarm and within moments, an army of CDA agents

rushed over to Mike's work station and destroyed the suspect object.

"False alarm! It was only an apple!" said one of the CDA agents.

"It's better to be safe than sorry," replied the CDA agent in charge.

"Wow! Those guys sure are thorough," gasped Sulley, as the CDA agents disappeared. Even though the muscles in Mike's face ached, he couldn't help grinning.

The following Sunday, Sulley got up early, ready to spend another hard day trying to get rid of the weeds in the garden.

"Relax, Sulley, our gardeners will be here soon," laughed Mike.

"Our gardeners?" puzzled Sulley.

Mike walked into the garden and pointed to the tall patch of weeds. "A CHILD! I THINK I SEE A HUMAN CHILD!" he shouted as loudly as he could.

Then all of a sudden, a CDA agent appeared, as if from nowhere, and sounded the alarm.

Seconds later, the huge decontamination squad piled into the garden and destroyed everything that could hide a child.

By the time they were finished, the weeds were all gone and the garden looked great.

"Oops, false alarm! I can't have seen a child, after all!" said Mike.

"It's better to be safe, than sorry," replied the CDA agent in charge.

When the CDA agents were gone, Mike was delighted. "No more aching muscles from pulling up weeds!" he cheerfully cried.

"We've still got one more job to do in the garden," said Sulley.

"What?" gulped Mike.

"We've got to put up our deckchairs so we can sunbathe!" laughed Sulley.

The end

Jelly jigglers

Mike is hanging out with his funny, wobbly friends! Here's how you can make another jelly monster to join their gang!

You will need: a packet of jelly, a measuring jug, a plastic cup, a plate, squirty cream, cherries, hundreds and thousands and a black icing pen.

1 Break up the jelly and put it into a measuring jug.

2 Ask an adult to help you mix up the jelly, using the instructions on the packet. Pour the jelly into a plastic cup. Wait for the jelly to set.

3 When the jelly has set, tip it out on to a plate.

Note to parents: adult supervision is recommended when boiling water is required.

4 Squirt on some cream for hair and push in some cherries for eyes.

5 Draw on some eyeballs and a big smile with a black icing pen.

NOW YOUR MONSTER IS READY TO JOIN HIS FRIENDS!

The great door chase

Randall is chasing Boo on a roller-coaster of swinging doors. Join the ride and unlock the answers to these crafty questions!

1 Which colour door is four from the left?

2 Which colour door appears at each end?

3 Unscramble the letters above the doors. What word do they spell?

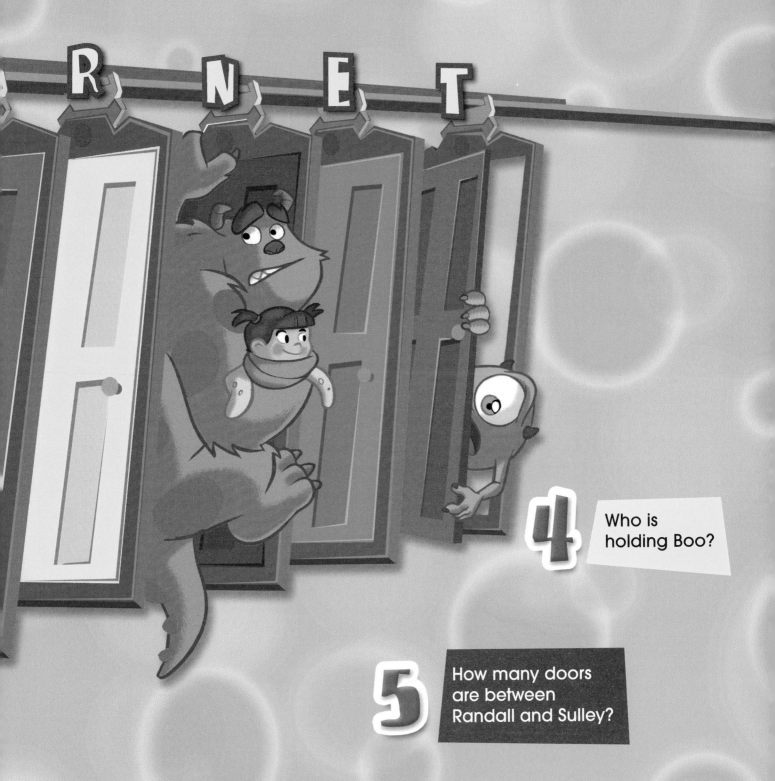

4 Who is holding Boo?

5 How many doors are between Randall and Sulley?

45

Take things easy

It was a beautiful, sunny day and the busy ants were collecting heavy sunflower seeds. "This sure is hard work," puffed Flik, as he staggered along with a huge seed.

"You should take the afternoon off and enjoy the sunshine," said a friendly voice. Flik looked up and saw a big snail.

"I'd love to take things easy, but we can't stop until we get all the seeds back to the colony," explained Flik.

"I can help you get them there in no time," smiled the snail.

"How?" asked Flik.

"Just follow my trail!" replied the rather large snail.

When the snail moved along, he left a slippery silver line behind him. Flik dropped his sunflower seed on to the trail and gave it a push. It slid along like a leaf on the wind.

The rest of the ants saw how easy this was and pushed their own sunflower seeds along the snail's trail.

Before long, all the seeds were at the colony door. "Thanks for your help," cheered the ants, as the snail moved off into the sunshine.

"No problem. Now you can take things easy," grinned the snail.

Suddenly, a shadow passed over

the ants and headed towards the snail. "Look out, there's a sparrow after you!" yelled Flik.

The snail saw the bird swooping and quickly retreated inside its shell. The sparrow pecked at the tough shell, but it couldn't get through. The ants sighed with relief, because they thought the snail was safe.

But the sparrow didn't go away. It kept flying around the snail, waiting for it to come out.

Flik shuddered every time the sparrow's shadow passed over him. "The sparrow knows the snail will have to move out of the hot sun before long!" cried Flik.

"But what can we do to help? The sparrow is so much bigger than any of us," said one of the other ants, with a great gulp.

"But he's not bigger than all of us together," said Flik. He told the army of ants to huddle together as tightly as they could. Then, he ran around the edge of the crowd, packing them into shape. "The only thing that'll scare a hungry sparrow, is an even hungrier sparrow hawk!" said Flik.

Flik led the shadow-shaped army towards the snail. When the sparrow looked down at the ground, it thought a real hawk was about to attack from behind. The terrified sparrow didn't bother looking back before darting off as fast as it could.

"Thanks for helping me," said the snail, as it moved to the safety of some cool leaves.

"No problem. Now we can all take things easy!" laughed Flik.

Atta's watch

At first glance, these two scenes may look identical but there are five differences in the lower one. Can you spot them all?

Answer: 1) First ant's grain has changed colour. 2) Second ant's eyes have changed colour. 3) A grain has appeared on the ground. 4) Third ant's antenna has changed direction. 5) Fourth ant's grain has changed colour.

Hungry Heimlich

Heimlich has taken a big bite out of Flik's weight! Use the bites at the bottom of the page to help you colour in this tasty picture.

Fun with Flik

Can you help Flik solve these three puzzles?

1 Using the letters below, how many times can you spell **ant**? You can only use each letter once.

2 What do the numbers on the leaves add up to?

3 Finish drawing this spider's web.

Answer: 1) 4. 2) 17.

Flik's Flight

Flik has invented a fantastic flying contraption. It's time for him to take his first test flight! Starting with picture a, put the pictures in order.

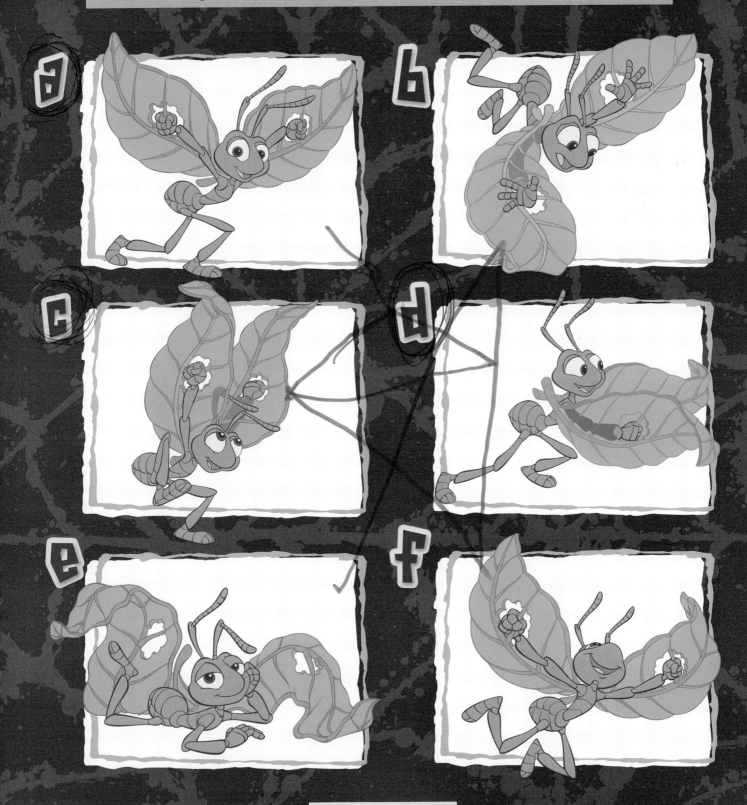

Answer: a,d,c,f,b,e.

Cool current

1

One afternoon, Dory and Nemo were taking Squirt home from school along the East Australian Current. Nemo was very excited to be going a different way home. "Mr Ray, the teacher, told us that the current is so strong that it makes us swim ten times faster than normal," Nemo told Dory. "Isn't it cool!" cheered Squirt, as he let the water tumble him over and over.

2

Suddenly, Squirt noticed an old shipwreck on the sea floor. "Wow! Look at that!" he gasped. Squirt broke away from the current and swam down to explore the shipwreck.

3

"Hey, Squirt! Wait for me!" shouted Nemo, as he turned and chased after him. "Who's Squirt?" asked Dory, forgetfully, as she followed Nemo down to the shipwreck.

4

"Look at all the cool things down here," said Squirt, as he swam around the shipwreck. Soon, Squirt caught sight of an old diving helmet and swam inside to investigate.

5

But as Squirt swam inside, his flipper knocked the front of the helmet and the grate snapped shut. "Help! I'm trapped!" cried Squirt, as Nemo and Dory rushed to help.

6

The two friends tried with all their strength to open the helmet but the grate was too heavy. "We're not strong enough to free Squirt! What are we going to do?" said Nemo.

7

Suddenly, Dory had an idea. "We're not strong enough but the current is!" she cried. Dory threaded some rope through the grate and told Nemo to take the other end into the current.

8

As soon as Nemo reached the current, it dragged him along at high speed. The current was so strong that it pulled the rope tight and the front of the helmet sprang open. "Thanks very much, Dory!" cried Squirt, as he swam out of the helmet. "What for?" asked Dory, as they all happily rejoined the East Australian Current and headed for home.

The end

About the story

1) What were Nemo, Dory and Squirt travelling along?
2) Who went to explore the shipwreck?
3) Where did Squirt get trapped?
4) What did Nemo and Dory use to free Squirt?
5) What type of creature is Squirt?

Answers:
1) The East Australian Current. 2) Squirt. 3) Inside a diving helmet.
4) Some rope and the East Australian Current. 5) A sea turtle.

Count for Dory

Dory is trying to count these colourful fish. Can you help her by writing the answer in the bubble next to each group?

55

Jumping jellyfish

Try playing this game with a friend and help Dory and Marlin through the jellyfish.

You will need: 2 counters and 1 dice.

Start

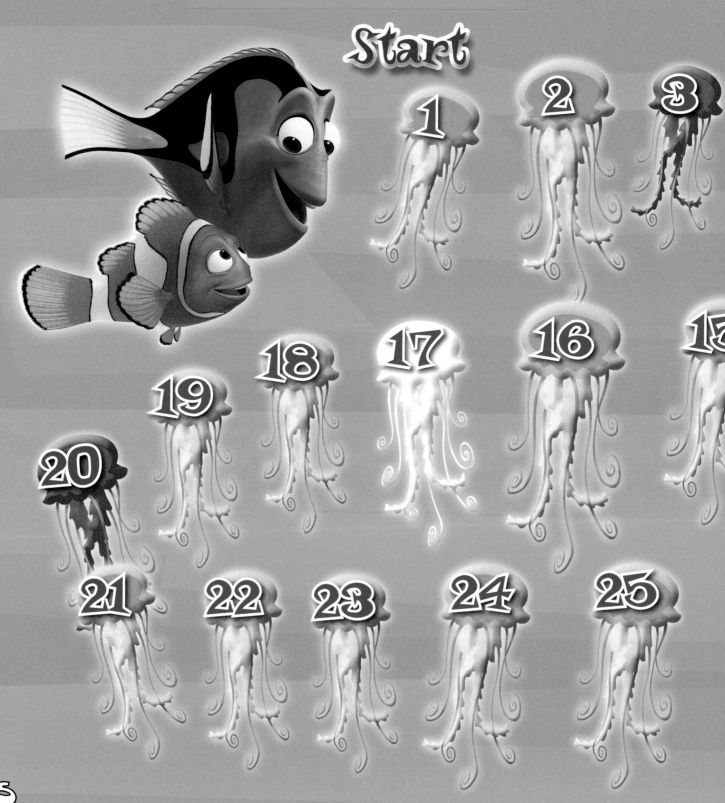

1   2   3

17   16   15

18

19

20

21   22   23   24   25

How to play

Roll the dice and move along the jellyfish.
Be careful of the white ones! If you land on
a white jellyfish then you have to miss a go.
The first player to the FINISH is the winner!

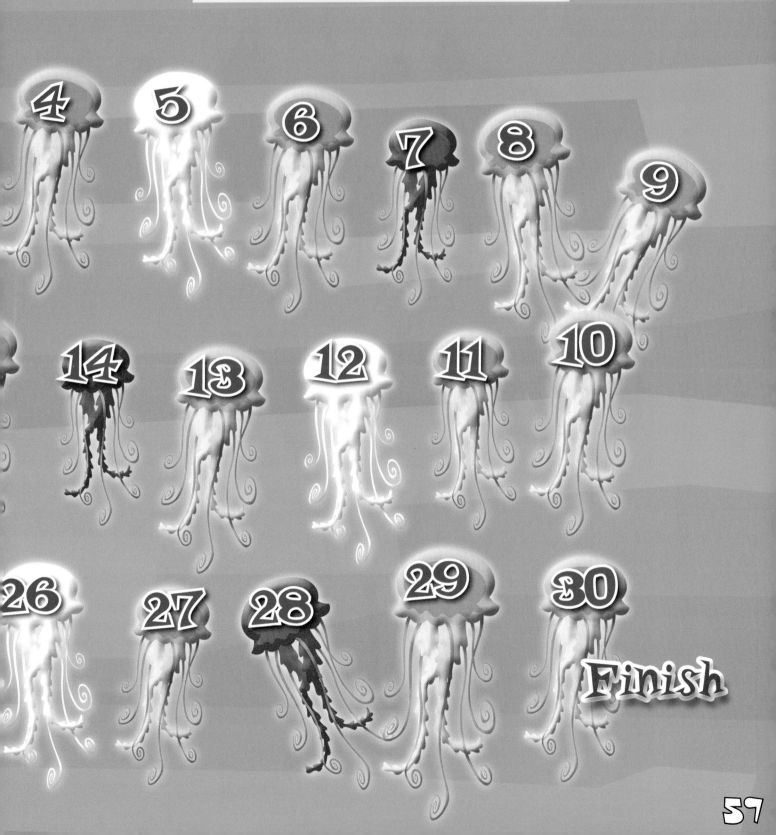

Tank Gang giggles

Gill and the Tank Gang are having fun. Why don't you join in by adding some colour to this picture?

Double take

At first glance, these two scenes may look identical but there are ten differences in the lower one. Can you spot them all?

59

Make a jellyfish

Here's how to make your very own wobbling jellyfish!

You will need: a paper plate, coloured tissue paper, white card, a length of elastic, a black pen, glue, scissors, tape and paint.

1 Cut a paper plate down the middle and paint one half red. This will be the body of the jellyfish.

2 Cut out several strips of different coloured tissue paper.

3 Tape the strips to the back of the body.

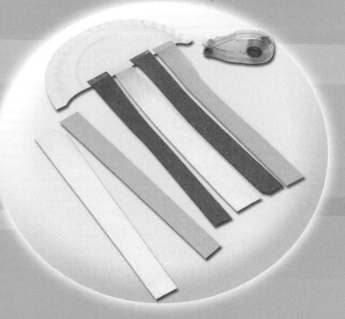

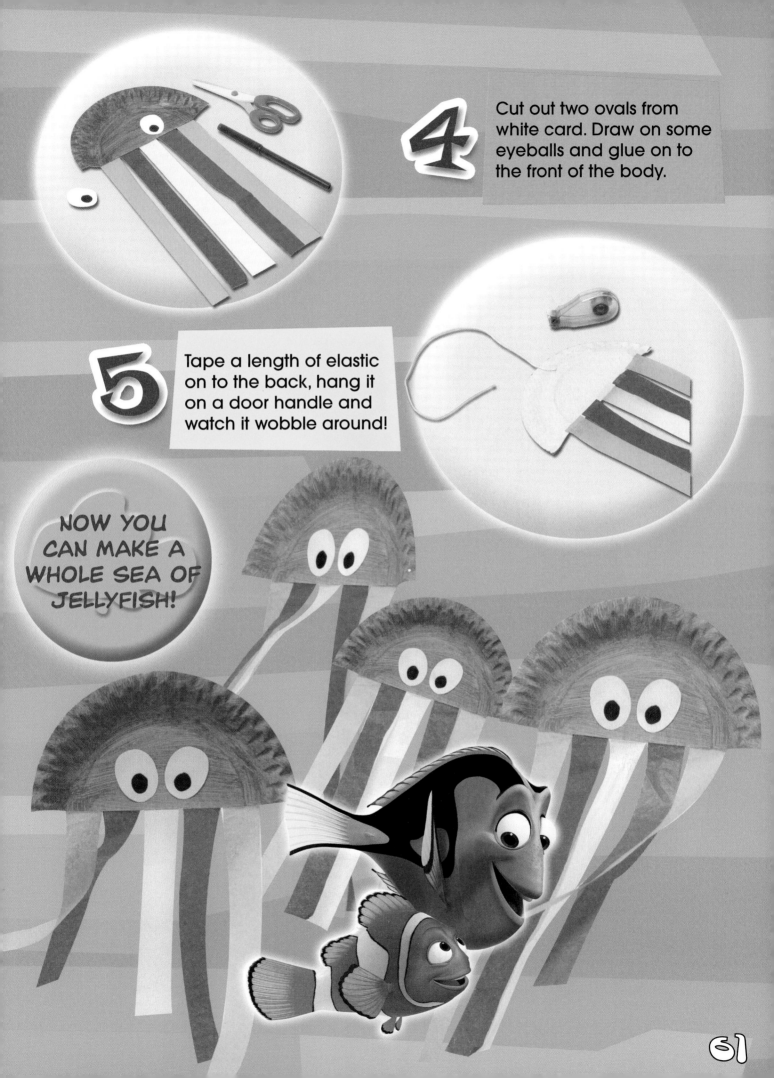

4 Cut out two ovals from white card. Draw on some eyeballs and glue on to the front of the body.

5 Tape a length of elastic on to the back, hang it on a door handle and watch it wobble around!

NOW YOU CAN MAKE A WHOLE SEA OF JELLYFISH!

Friendly fun

Nemo and his friends are playing at the Drop-off.
Why don't you join in the fun by answering these questions?

1 Who has swum out the furthest?

2 How many bubbles can you count?

3 Can you unscramble the letters on the coral to find the name of one of Nemo's friends?

Whose shape is hidden in the coral?

Who is swimming the highest?

How many eyes can you count on this page?

Ride the waves

Dory decides to spice up ocean life with a wild amusement park ride, sea-style! Will Marlin and Nemo climb aboard?

One morning, Dory and Marlin were swimming over the coral reef.

"I'm bored," sighed Dory. "Let's do something really exciting."

"All right," agreed Marlin. "What do you have in mind?"

"I think this ocean is missing an amusement park," said Dory. "So, let's create our own ride!"

Marlin shuddered with fright.

"Don't worry," said Dory. "The ride won't be too scary."

Nemo was away at school, so Marlin agreed. He followed her down a very long, dark tube into the centre of the coral reef.

"Now, we wait," whispered Dory.

"Wait for what?" asked Marlin.

"Shh, I can hear it rumbling," Dory whispered again.

Sure enough, there was a rumbling noise. First it was very quiet, then it became louder and louder until it was right behind them.

"Brace yourself!" shouted Dory, with a huge smile on her face.

"Can I get off this ride, please?" begged Marlin. But it was too late. As Marlin glanced behind him, he saw a great jet of water come shooting towards him.

"Keep your hands away from the walls and please stow any cameras and bags!" shouted Dory.

Then, like a volcano erupting, Dory and Marlin were catapulted along the tube, through the water and high into the sky.

"Yahoo!" screamed Dory. "This is a great ride."

"I think I'm going to be sick," cried Marlin, as he was sent tumbling through the air.

Suddenly, the jet of water fell away and Dory and Marlin plummeted back into the ocean.

Just then, Mr Ray appeared, followed by Nemo and the other schoolchildren.

Dory told Nemo and the others all about their ride on the giant jet of water. "You weren't scared were you, Dad?" asked Nemo.

"Err ... no ... of course not," replied Marlin, trying to put on a brave face.

"I've never been on a ride, Dad," said Nemo. "Can I go on the water jet ride, too?"

Marlin didn't want to stop Nemo from doing anything but the ride was very scary. Mr Ray could see that Marlin was worried and he spoke up. "Hey, Nemo, I know of an even better ride than the water jet ride," he said. "It's called Rollercoaster Ray!"

"Wow! Can I go on the Rollercoaster Ray ride, Dad? Please?" begged Nemo.

"Well, all right," smiled Marlin.

"All aboard," called Mr Ray, as the children climbed on excitedly.

"All ready?" shouted Mr Ray, as he waved his tail. "OK, then hold on tight and off we go!"

Mr Ray dived down, spiralling through the water. He twisted and turned and even did a loop-the-loop!

"I definitely prefer watching a ride to being on one," chuckled Marlin.

The end

65

Dodge the diver

Nemo is busy trying to get away from the diver. Can you help Marlin reach him before the diver does? Remember to watch out for the bubbles!

The jellyfish game

Can you help Dory jump across the jellyfish to reach Marlin safely? She must start with the lowest number and jump in order across the jellyfish to the highest number.

What do you know?

Answer each statement by ticking the box TRUE or FALSE. Then, check the answers at the bottom to see how many you got right. Good luck!

1 Slim is a stick insect. □ TRUE □ FALSE

2 Flik loves Princess Atta. □ TRUE □ FALSE

3 Francis is a female ladybird □ TRUE □ FALSE

4 Tuck and Roll are performing lizards. □ TRUE □ FALSE

5 Elastigirl is married to Mr. Incredible. □ TRUE □ FALSE

6 Violet is Dash's older sister. □ TRUE □ FALSE

7 Edna Mode is stronger than Mr. Incredible. □ TRUE □ FALSE

8 Dash can freeze water. □ TRUE □ FALSE

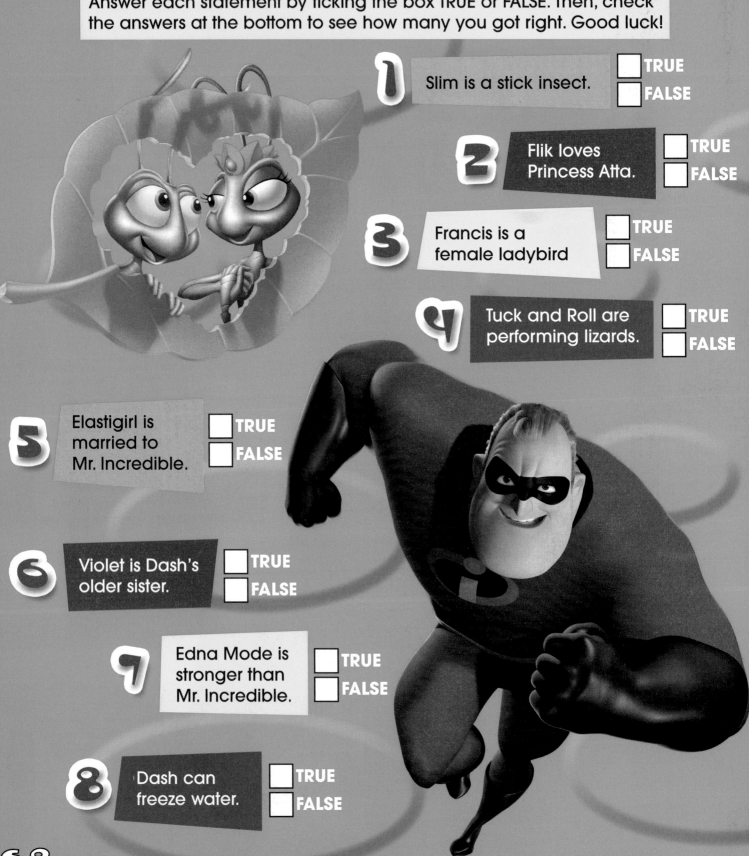

9 Bruce is a singing jellyfish. ☐ TRUE ☐ FALSE

10 Marlin is Nemo's father. ☐ TRUE ☐ FALSE

11 Dory forgets things she's just done or said. ☐ TRUE ☐ FALSE

12 Nemo is an orange clownfish. ☐ TRUE ☐ FALSE

13 Rex is a red dinosaur. ☐ TRUE ☐ FALSE

14 Woody is a toy pirate. ☐ TRUE ☐ FALSE

15 Hamm is a toy piggy bank. ☐ TRUE ☐ FALSE

16 Buzz has wings that pop out. ☐ TRUE ☐ FALSE

17 Sulley's real name is James P. Sullivan. ☐ TRUE ☐ FALSE

18 Boo can make herself disappear. ☐ TRUE ☐ FALSE

19 Mike is in love with Celia. ☐ TRUE ☐ FALSE

20 Randall is furry. ☐ TRUE ☐ FALSE

Answer:
1) TRUE. 2) TRUE. 3) FALSE. 4) FALSE. 5) TRUE.
6) TRUE. 7) FALSE. 8) FALSE. 9) FALSE. 10) TRUE.
11) TRUE. 12) TRUE. 13) FALSE. 14) FALSE. 15) TRUE.
16) TRUE. 17) TRUE. 18) FALSE. 19) TRUE. 20) FALSE.

69

Disney · PIXAR